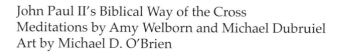

John Paul II's Biblical Way of the Cross
Meditations by Amy Welborn and Michael Dubruiel
Art by Michael D. O'Brien

Founded in 1865, Ave Maria Press is a ministry of the Indiana Prov-
ince of Holy Cross.

www.avemariapress.com

ISBN-10 1-59471-128-3   ISBN-13 978-1-59471-128-2

Cover design by Katharine Cummins.

Text design by K. H. Coney.

Cover and interior artwork © Michael D. O'Brien

Printed and bound in the United States of America.

Introduction

The Way of the Cross has been an integral part of the devotional life of Catholics for centuries. The roots of the devotion can be found in the early Christian practice of retracing the path Jesus walked from the genesis of his passion in the Garden of Gethsemane on the Mount of Olives, through the Valley of Kidron, along the streets of Jerusalem, and finally to the summit of Calvary. This ancient path of pilgrimage was more inclusive of the entire passion of Christ than later versions. Rather than beginning in the Garden of Gethsemane, later versions, including the arrangement found in most Catholic churches today, begin with the condemnation of Jesus and include a number of stations that are based more on tradition than on the scriptures.

In 1991, Pope John Paul II introduced a new version of the Way of the Cross that follows the more ancient practice. Pope Benedict XVI has continued it. This "new" scriptural version is presented here, fully developed for parish or individual use. These stations are listed on the inside of the front cover, and a quick review illustrates the similarities and differences between the traditional fourteen stations and these scriptural stations.

John Paul II's Biblical Way of the Cross is composed in a liturgical format, using responses and ministries evocative of those experienced during the eucharistic liturgy. It offers an opportunity for many to be involved in helping to lead the assembly in prayer: a lector to proclaim the scripture passage, a leader (either lay or ordained) to offer the meditation, and a cantor or choir to lead the assembly in singing the "Lord Have Mercy" as a penitential response after each station as well as an appropriate hymn between the stations.

This version of the stations is ideal for individual or group use in the parish. Fourteen prayer sites within the church are suggested for the fourteen Biblical stations. Parishioners are therefore able to move from one station site to another, though these sites will not duplicate the traditional station sequence. Parishioners can also participate in this rich devotion by remaining seated in the pews, accompanying Jesus in spirit and prayer on this Biblical Way of the Cross.

Because it is based wholly on scripture, these stations are ideal for use with ecumenical groups. This devotion is also ripe with catechetical possibilities for youth. Catechists might consider designing a Lenten mini-course, based on *John Paul II's Biblical Way of the Cross*. It could expose youth to serious scripture study and reflection on the meaning of the passion in their own lives. The youth could also help direct this devotion for the whole parish.

Praying *John Paul II's Biblical Way of the Cross* can lead to an experience of the deep love of God revealed through the suffering and death of the Lord. It can also provide an opportunity for reflection on how God's love is revealed through our experiences of loss, betrayal, and death. Praying these stations, whether in private or as a public prayer, should help a person draw closer to Jesus Christ. It is our hope that as you follow this Way of the Cross you will experience the same certitude of faith in the love that God has for you as Jesus did when he accepted his cross, and that you will be rewarded with a share in his resurrection.

Amy Welborn and Michael Dubruiel

The First Station

JESUS PRAYS IN THE GARDEN

Station Site: Main Entrance to the Church or Outdoors at Suitable Site

Leader: We praise you, Jesus, and give you thanks!

People: By your cross and resurrection you have set us free!

Lector: A reading from the Gospel of Luke. (Lk 22:41–46)

Then he withdrew from them about a stone's throw, knelt down, and prayed, "Father, if you are willing, remove this cup from me; yet, not my will but yours be done." Then an angel from heaven appeared to him and gave him strength. In his anguish he prayed more earnestly, and his sweat became like great drops of blood falling down on the ground. When he got up from prayer, he came to the disciples and found them sleeping because of grief, and he said to them, "Why are you sleeping? Get up and pray that you may not come into the time of trial."

All Kneel

Leader: Jesus, we see you in the garden, praying in the darkness of night. Your anguished prayer is one of deep struggle with the Father's will. While you agonize over the Father's will and are strengthened to fulfill his plan, your disciples, overcome with sadness, can do nothing but give themselves over to sleep. As we begin this journey with you, Jesus, help us to see that for you it was a journey of love. May we learn from this walk how to follow you more closely and accept the love that you have for us.

People: O Jesus, wake us from our sleep. Help us to face life's difficulties honestly, knowing that we can trust in God. Strengthen us in the time of our trials. May our prayer always be an expression of all that we are, and all that we do. We love you, Jesus; teach us how to pray.

All Stand

Leader: Lord, have mercy.   **People:** Lord, have mercy.

Leader: Christ, have mercy.   **People:** Christ, have mercy.

Leader: Lord, have mercy.   **People:** Lord, have mercy.

The Second Station

JESUS IS BETRAYED AND ARRESTED

Station Site: Halfway Up the Middle Aisle

Leader: We praise you, Jesus, and give you thanks!

People: By your cross and resurrection you have set us free!

Lector: A reading from the Gospel of Mark. (Mk 14:43–46)

Immediately, while [Jesus] was still speaking, Judas, one of the twelve, arrived; and with him there was a crowd with swords and clubs, from the chief priests, the scribes, and the elders. Now the betrayer had given them a sign, saying, "The one I will kiss is the man; arrest him and lead him away under guard." So when he came, he went up to him at once and said, "Rabbi!" and kissed him. Then they laid hands on him and arrested him.

All Kneel

Leader: Jesus, as you wake your disciples, one who has not slept arrives with an angry crowd. Judas reveals your identity to them with a kiss. His act of affection is a signal to point you out as the one who loves but is rejected by his own.

People: O Jesus, we are quick to greet you with affection in our prayer and worship. But how often do our external words and actions conceal hearts that are easily turned from you? We love you, Jesus, help us to love you with all of our hearts.

All Stand

Leader: Lord, have mercy.   **People:** Lord, have mercy.

Leader: Christ, have mercy.   **People:** Christ, have mercy.

Leader: Lord, have mercy.   **People:** Lord, have mercy.

The Third Station

JESUS IS CONDEMNED BY THE SANHEDRIN

Station Site: At the Foot of the Altar

Leader: We praise you, Jesus, and give you thanks!

People: By your cross and resurrection you have set us free!

Lector: A reading from the Gospel of Matthew. (Mt 26:62–66)

The high priest stood up and said, "Have you no answer? What is it that they testify against you?" But Jesus was silent. Then the high priest said to him, "I put you under oath before the living God, tell us if you are the Messiah, the Son of God." Jesus said to him, "You have said so. But I tell you, from now on you will see the Son of Man seated at the right hand of power and coming on the clouds of heaven." Then the high priest tore his clothes and said, "He has blasphemed! Why do we still need witnesses? You have now heard his blasphemy. What is your verdict?" They answered, "He deserves death."

All Kneel

Leader: Jesus, your words are blasphemy to the ears of the high priest. He tears his garments, unable to see the presence of God in the one who stands before him arrested and accused. He cannot believe in a God who, because of such great love, would willingly become so powerless.

People: O Jesus, we can be so limited in our vision. We find it difficult to look beyond our narrow expectations and see you as you are. Give us the grace to hear your words clearly and to follow you in truth. We love you, Jesus; reveal to us what God is like.

All Stand

Leader: Lord, have mercy.	**People:** Lord, have mercy.
Leader: Christ, have mercy.	**People:** Christ, have mercy.
Leader: Lord, have mercy.	**People:** Lord, have mercy.

The Fourth Station

PETER DENIES KNOWING JESUS

Station Site: Near a Side Entrance or Side Altar

Leader: We praise you, Jesus, and give you thanks!

People: By your cross and resurrection you have set us free!

Lector: A reading from the Gospel of Matthew. (Mt 26:69–75)

Now Peter was sitting outside in the courtyard. A servant-girl came to him and said, "You also were with Jesus the Galilean." But he denied it before all of them, saying, "I do not know what you are talking about." When he went out to the porch, another servant-girl saw him, and she said to the bystanders, "This man was with Jesus of Nazareth." Again he denied it with an oath, "I do not know the man." After a little while the bystanders came up and said to Peter, "Certainly you are also one of them, for your accent betrays you." Then he began to curse, and he swore an oath, "I do not know the man!" At that moment the cock crowed. Then Peter remembered what Jesus had said: "Before the cock crows, you will deny me three times." And he went out and wept bitterly.

All Kneel

Leader: Jesus, you told Peter that he would deny you three times before the cock would crow. He did not believe you. He swore that he would never deny you, and that in fact he was willing to die for you. Peter felt that he knew himself better than you knew him. But now as dawn approaches and the cock crows, he sees the truth.

People: O Jesus, we set out to follow you but then quickly turn, going our own way. We are afraid to acknowledge you in front of others, but you speak to us in the midst of our denial. We love you, Jesus; keep us faithful to you.

All Stand

Leader: Lord, have mercy.   **People:** Lord, have mercy.

Leader: Christ, have mercy.   **People:** Christ, have mercy.

Leader: Lord, have mercy.   **People:** Lord, have mercy.

The Fifth Station

JESUS IS CONDEMNED BY PILATE

Station Site: Station 1 — Jesus Is Condemned

Leader: We praise you, Jesus, and give you thanks!

People: By your cross and resurrection you have set us free!

Lector: A reading from the Gospel of Luke. (Lk 23:13–15, 23–24)

Pilate then called together the chief priests, the leaders, and the People, and said to them, "You brought me this man as one who was perverting the People; and here I have examined him in your presence and have not found this man guilty of any of your charges against him. Neither has Herod, for he has sent him back to us. Indeed, he has done nothing to deserve death."

But they kept urgently demanding with loud shouts that he be crucified; and their voices prevailed. So Pilate gave his verdict that their demand should be granted.

All Kneel

Leader: Jesus, Pilate perceives your innocence, but the crowd insists on guilt. Hearing their persistent shouts, Pilate sets aside the judgment of his conscience, and the decision is made. He hands you over to be crucified.

People: O Jesus, how often do we let the threatening voice of the crowd overwhelm the voice of conscience? Fill us with compassion for the outcast and commitment to the truth. We love you, Jesus; lead us beyond the crowd.

All Stand

Leader: Lord, have mercy.   **People:** Lord, have mercy.

Leader: Christ, have mercy.   **People:** Christ, have mercy.

Leader: Lord, have mercy.   **People:** Lord, have mercy.

The Sixth Station

JESUS IS SCOURGED AND CROWNED WITH THORNS

Station Site: Between Stations 1 and 2

Leader: We praise you, Jesus, and give you thanks!

People: By your cross and resurrection you have set us free!

Lector: A reading from the Gospel of Mark. (Mk 15:16–19)

Then the soldiers led him into the courtyard of the palace (that is the governor's headquarters); and they called together the whole cohort. And they clothed him in a purple cloak; and after twisting some thorns into a crown, they put it on him. And they began saluting him, "Hail, King of the Jews!" They struck his head with a reed, spat upon him, and knelt down in homage to him.

All Kneel

Leader: Jesus, soldiers of an earthly realm mock your kingship. You are so powerless in their eyes, so weak, the ruler of a kingdom that cannot be seen, and, therefore, must not exist. They treat you as a foolish imposter, caught in a lie.

People: O Jesus, how often do we look for the kingdom with the eyes of the world rather than with the eyes of faith. We forget your promise that your kingdom is among us. Help us to see your strength in our weakness, your reign in our powerlessness. We love you, Jesus; establish your rule over us.

All Stand

Leader: Lord, have mercy. **People:** Lord, have mercy.

Leader: Christ, have mercy. **People:** Christ, have mercy.

Leader: Lord, have mercy. **People:** Lord, have mercy.

The Seventh Station

Jesus Takes up His Cross

Station Site: Station 2 — Jesus Takes Up His Cross

Leader: We praise you, Jesus, and give you thanks!

People: By your cross and resurrection you have set us free!

Lector: A reading from the Gospel of John. (Jn 19:16b–17)

Then [Pilate] handed [Jesus] over to [the Jews] to be crucified. So they took Jesus; and carrying the cross by himself, he went out to what is called The Place of the Skull, which in Hebrew is called Golgotha.

All Kneel

Leader: Jesus, like Isaac carrying the wood to the mountain, you set out with the wood of the cross. But unlike him you will not ask your Father where the lamb is, because you know you are the lamb of the sacrifice. You now begin your journey with the cross.

People: O Jesus, you carry a cross, which is given unjustly. You willingly bear the burden of our sinfulness and accept the cross of our guilt. There is no greater love than this, to lay down one's life for one's friends. We love you, Jesus; help us to show this love in our lives.

All Stand

Leader: Lord, have mercy.	**People:** Lord, have mercy.
Leader: Christ, have mercy.	**People:** Christ, have mercy.
Leader: Lord, have mercy.	**People:** Lord, have mercy.

The Eighth Station

SIMON OF CYRENE HELPS JESUS

Station Site: Station 5 — Simon Helps Jesus

Leader: We praise you, Jesus, and give you thanks!

People: By your cross and resurrection you have set us free!

Lector: A reading from the Gospel of Luke. (Lk 23:26)

As they led him away, they seized a man, Simon of Cyrene, who was coming from the country, and they laid the cross on him, and made him carry it behind Jesus.

All Kneel

Leader: Jesus, the torture you experienced at the hands of the soldiers left you weak. When you prayed in the garden that the will of the Father be done, an angel was sent to strengthen you. Now, as you seek to fulfill the Father's will, he sends Simon to help you.

People: O Jesus, strengthen us on our journey. Open our hearts to the help you offer through the kindness of others. Open our eyes to the needs of those who walk beside us. We love you, Jesus; lighten our burdens.

All Stand

Leader: Lord, have mercy.   **People:** Lord, have mercy.

Leader: Christ, have mercy.   **People:** Christ, have mercy.

Leader: Lord, have mercy.   **People:** Lord, have mercy.

The Ninth Station

JESUS MEETS THE WEEPING WOMEN

Station Site: Station 8 — Jesus Meets the Women of Jerusalem

Leader: We praise you, Jesus, and give you thanks!

People: By your cross and resurrection you have set us free!

Lector: A reading from the Gospel of Luke. (Lk 23:27–31)

A great number of People followed him, and among them were women who were beating their breasts and wailing for him. But Jesus turned to them and said, "Daughters of Jerusalem, do not weep for me, but weep for yourselves and your children. For the days are surely coming when they will say, 'Blessed are the barren, and the wombs that never bore, and the breasts that never nursed.' Then they will begin to say to the mountains, 'Fall on us'; and to the hills, 'Cover us.' For if they do this when the wood is green, what will happen when it is dry?"

All Kneel

Leader: Jesus, after being silent, you speak. You turn the eyes of the women away from your suffering and toward the destructive powers of sin. You warn them not to shed their tears for you but rather for themselves and their children. If you, the innocent one, can suffer so, what will be the fate of the guilty?

People: O Jesus, the wood is now very dry! Set fire to the world so that it might burn with your love. Destroy all hatred, fill us with joy again. Teach us to mourn the way things are; show us the way they could be. We love you, Jesus; weep for us.

All Stand

Leader: Lord, have mercy.   **People:** Lord, have mercy.

Leader: Christ, have mercy.   **People:** Christ, have mercy.

Leader: Lord, have mercy.   **People:** Lord, have mercy.

The Tenth Station

JESUS IS CRUCIFIED

Station Site: Station 11 — Jesus Is Crucified

Leader: We praise you, Jesus, and give you thanks!

People: By your cross and resurrection you have set us free!

Lector: A reading from the Gospel of Luke. (Lk 23:33–38)

When they came to the place that is called The Skull, they crucified Jesus there with the criminals, one on his right and one on his left. Then Jesus said, "Father, forgive them; for they do not know what they are doing." And they cast lots to divide his clothing. And the People stood by, watching; but the leaders scoffed at him, saying, "He saved others; let him save himself if he is the Messiah of God, his chosen one!" The soldiers also mocked him, coming up and offering him sour wine, and saying, "If you are the King of the Jews, save yourself!" There was also an inscription over him, "This is the King of the Jews."

All Kneel

Leader: Jesus, your suffering continues as nails are driven into your hands and feet and taunting jeers are hurled at your body imprisoned on the cross. Yet to those who mock and challenge you, you offer no reproach, only forgiveness and compassion for them in their ignorance.

People: O Jesus, how often we have acted as if the way of the cross were unnecessary and too difficult. We believe we know a better way, a way worn down by the crowd. We find that path goes nowhere. Forgive us; we do not know what we are doing. We love you, Jesus; by your wounds heal us.

All Stand

Leader: Lord, have mercy.   **People:** Lord, have mercy.

Leader: Christ, have mercy.   **People:** Christ, have mercy.

Leader: Lord, have mercy.   **People:** Lord, have mercy.

The Eleventh Station

JESUS PROMISES PARADISE
TO THE CRUCIFIED THIEF

Station Site: Between Stations 11 and 12

Leader: We praise you, Jesus, and give you thanks!

People: By your cross and resurrection you have set us free!

Lector: A reading from the Gospel of Luke. (Lk 23:39–43)

One of the criminals who were hanged there kept deriding [Jesus] saying, "Are you not the Messiah? Save yourself and us!" But the other rebuked him saying, "Do you not fear God, since you are under the same sentence of condemnation? And we indeed have been condemned justly, for we are getting what we deserve for our deeds, but this man has done nothing wrong." Then he said, "Jesus, remember me when you come into your kingdom." He replied, "Truly I tell you, today you will be with me in Paradise."

All Kneel

Leader: Jesus, two others are nailed on either side of you. One challenges you to release him now; the other asks to be freed with you in your kingdom. One sees only weakness; the other sees power and is able to trust in a promise of everlasting life with you as his time in this world comes to an end.

People: O Jesus, look upon us now. See us in our need and hear us as we cry out to you. Help us to trust you in difficult circumstances. Give us eyes to see your power in hopeless times, to see your kingdom in all we encounter. We love you, Jesus; remember us.

All Stand

Leader: Lord, have mercy.   **People:** Lord, have mercy.

Leader: Christ, have mercy.   **People:** Christ, have mercy.

Leader: Lord, have mercy.   **People:** Lord, have mercy.

The Twelfth Station

JESUS CARES FOR HIS MOTHER

Station Site: Station 4 — Jesus Meets His Mother

Leader: We praise you, Jesus, and give you thanks!

People: By your cross and resurrection you have set us free!

Lector: A reading from the Gospel of John. (Jn 19:25–27)

Standing near the cross of Jesus were his mother, and his mother's sister, Mary the wife of Clopas, and Mary Magdalene. When Jesus saw his mother and the disciple whom he loved standing beside her, he said to his mother, "Woman, here is your son." Then he said to the disciple, "Here is your mother." And from that hour the disciple took her into his own home.

All Kneel

Leader: Jesus, you give your mother to the disciple you love. Even as you face death, you entrust those whom you love most into each other's care. Your dying is marked by giving, and by concern for the ones who remain. You do not leave us as orphans, you have promised your Spirit to your church, and at the cross the church is born.

People: O Jesus, help us see that we are the disciples you love, and you have given Mary, your mother, to us, too. We pray that we might allow the Spirit to give us life as sisters and brothers joined in mutual care. We love you, Jesus; bind us as one.

All Stand

Leader: Lord, have mercy.　　**People:** Lord, have mercy.

Leader: Christ, have mercy.　　**People:** Christ, have mercy.

Leader: Lord, have mercy.　　**People:** Lord, have mercy.

The Thirteenth Station

Jesus Dies

Station Site: Station 12 – Jesus Dies

Leader: We praise you, Jesus, and give you thanks!

People: By your cross and resurrection you have set us free!

Lector: A reading from the Gospel of Luke. (Lk 23:44–47)

It was now about noon, and darkness came over the whole land until three in the afternoon, while the sun's light failed; and the curtain of the temple was torn in two. Then Jesus, crying with a loud voice, said, "Father, into your hands I commend my spirit." Having said this, he breathed his last. When the centurion saw what had taken place, he praised God and said, "Certainly this man was innocent."

All Kneel

Leader: Jesus, the Word spoken by the Father, you now return to him, having accomplished the purpose for which you were sent. Your trust in the Father remains, even amid the dark clouds of death.

People: O Jesus, may we too accomplish the purpose for which we were created. Help us to commit ourselves into the Father's hands, to trust in him, and believe in his love for us, a love that your death reveals to us. May your dying never be in vain. We love you, Jesus; help us to die to ourselves and live for you.

All Stand

Leader: Lord, have mercy.   **People:** Lord, have mercy.

Leader: Christ, have mercy.   **People:** Christ, have mercy.

Leader: Lord, have mercy.   **People:** Lord, have mercy.

The Fourteenth Station

JESUS IS BURIED

Station Site: Station 14 — Jesus Is Buried

Leader: We praise you, Jesus, and give you thanks!

People: By your cross and resurrection you have set us free!

Lector: A reading from the Gospel of Luke. (Lk 23:53–56)

Then [Joseph of Arimathea] took [the body of Jesus] down, wrapped it in a linen cloth, and laid it in a rock-hewn tomb where no one had ever been laid. It was the day of Preparation, and the sabbath was beginning. The women who had come with him from Galilee followed, and they saw the tomb and how his body was laid. Then they returned, and prepared spices and ointments. On the sabbath they rested according to the commandment.

All Kneel

Leader: Jesus, now the time of surrender, of being at rest, begins. It is the seventh day when God rested from the work of creation. And you, the Son of God, rest and await the dawn of the eighth day when all will be made new—and we wait with you.

People: O Jesus, teach us to rest. Deliver us from thinking that everything depends upon our actions. Help us to be patient in trusting that God will bring about the completion of his creation through you. We love you, Jesus; fill us with your peace.

All Stand

Leader: Lord, have mercy.   **People:** Lord, have mercy.

Leader: Christ, have mercy.   **People:** Christ, have mercy.

Leader: Lord, have mercy.   **People:** Lord, have mercy.

Closing Prayer

Lector: A reading from the Gospel of John. (Jn 20:19–21)

When it was evening on that day, the first day of the week, and the doors of the house where the disciples had met were locked for fear of the Jews, Jesus came and stood among them and said, "Peace be with you." After he said this, he showed them his hands and his side. Then the disciples rejoiced when they saw the Lord. Jesus said to them again, "Peace be with you. As the Father has sent me, so I send you."

All Kneel

Leader: Jesus, with joy we view your victorious wounds. Help us to meditate on them and to see in them the sign of victory. May they give us courage to go forth with your blessing.

People: O Jesus, bless us with your outstretched hands. Give us your peace, give us your love. We love you, Jesus; be with us as we go out to do the will of God in our lives.